THEMATIC UN[IT]
Gingerbread

Written by Daphne Ransom

Teacher Created Materials, Inc.
6421 Industry Way
Westminster, CA 92683
www.teachercreated.com
©2001 Teacher Created Materials, Inc.
Made in U.S.A.

ISBN-0-7439-3101-7

Editor
Mara Ellen Guckian

Contributing Editor
Janet A. Hale, M.S. Ed.

Illustrated by
Bruce Hedges

Cover Art by
Barb Lorseyedi

Table of Contents

Introduction

Gingerbread is a captivating, comprehensive, language-based, thematic unit. Its 80 exciting pages are filled with a wide variety of cross-the-curriculum lesson ideas designed for use with primary-aged children. At its core are two high-quality children's literature selections: *The Gingerbread Boy* and *Gingerbread Baby*. Also included is a mini-book, *Let's Make a Gingerbread House*. For these selections, activities are included that set the stage for reading, encourage the enjoyment of the books, and extend the concepts gained. In addition, the theme is connected to the curriculum with activities in language arts, math, science, social studies, art, music, and life skills. Suggestions and patterns for bulletin boards are additional timesavers for the busy teacher.

This thematic unit includes the following:

- ❏ **literature selections**—summaries of two children's books and a mini-book with related lessons (complete with reproducible pages) that cross the curriculum

- ❏ **planning guides**—suggestions for sequencing lessons each day of the unit

- ❏ **curriculum connections**—in language arts, math, science, social studies, art, music, life skills, and physical education

- ❏ **group projects**—to foster cooperative learning

- ❏ **culminating activities**—which require children to synthesize their learning to produce a product or engage in an activity that can be shared with others

- ❏ **"gingerlinks"**—Web links to gain additional information about unit topics

- ❏ **bibliography of related reading**—suggestions for additional books on the theme

---

To keep this valuable resource intact so that it can be used year after year, you may wish to punch holes in the pages and store them in a three-ring binder.

Introduction *(cont.)*

Why a Balanced Approach?

The strength of a balanced language approach is that it involves children in using all modes of communication—reading, writing, listening, illustrating, and doing. Communication skills are interconnected and integrated into lessons that emphasize the whole of language. Implicit in this approach is our knowledge that every whole—including individual words—is composed of parts, and directed study of those parts can help a child to master the whole. Experience and research tell us that regular attention to phonics, other word-attack skills, spelling, etc., develops reading mastery, thereby fulfilling the unity of the whole-language experience. The child is thus led to read, write, spell, speak, and listen more confidently in response to a literature experience introduced by the teacher. In these ways, language skills grow rapidly, stimulated by direct practice, involvement, and interest in the topic.

Why Thematic Planning?

One very useful tool for implementing an integrated whole-language program is thematic planning. By choosing a theme with correlating literature selections for a unit of study, a teacher can plan activities throughout the day that lead to a cohesive, in-depth study of the topic. Children will be practicing and applying their skills in meaningful contexts. Consequently, they will tend to learn and retain more.

Why Cooperative Learning?

Besides academic skills and content, children need to learn social skills. No longer can this area of development be taken for granted. Children must learn to work cooperatively in groups in order to function well in modern society. Group activities should be a regular part of school life and teachers should consciously include social objectives, as well as academic objectives, in their planning.

Why Journals?

Each day your children should have the opportunity to write in a journal. They may respond to a book or an event in history, write about a personal experience, or answer a general "question of the day" posed by the teacher. The culminating journal provides an excellent means of documenting a child's writing process.

Why Big Books?

An excellent cooperative, whole language acrivity is the production of big books. Groups of children, or the whole class, can apply their language skills, content knowledge, and creativity to produce a big book that becomes a part of the classroom library to be read and reread. These books make an excellent culminating projects for sharing beyond the classroom with parents, librarians, other classes, etc.

The Gingerbread Boy

by Paul Galdone

Summary

The Gingerbread Boy is a delightful folk tale originating in North America. The clever, little Gingerbread Boy runs away from a host of hungry characters including his makers, the little old woman and little old man. The story ends when the Gingerbread Boy meets someone who's more clever than he—Mr. Fox.

The outline below is a suggested plan for using various activities that are presented in this unit.

Sample Plan

Lesson 1

- Introduce and read *The Gingerbread Boy* (page 6, Setting the Stage, #3).
- Create a gingerbread kids garland (page 10, #9).

Lesson 2

- Read the story focusing on the sequence of events. (page 7, Enjoying the Book, #4).
- Play "Who Stole the Cookie from the Cookie Jar?" (page 9, #2).
- Pictorially sequence *The Gingerbread Boy* (page 7, #4).

Lesson 3

- Retell the story (page 8, #6).
- Teach the song, "Come Back Little Man" (page 61).
- Play the Character Game (page 65).
- Make a song wheel (pages 13–14).

Lesson 4

- Read other versions of the story (page 10, #6).
- Complete the Venn diagram (page 16).
- Teach or review addition and subtraction concepts (page 9, #1).
- Create pop-up books (page 9, #1).

Lesson 5

- Have a Gingerbread Boy Hunt (page 8, Enjoying the Book, #5).
- Complete an origami project (page 60).

Overview of Activities

Setting the Stage

1. Collect a variety of gingerbread-man cookie cutters in various sizes and shapes. Place them in a learning-center area with modeling clay. Allow free or planned time for your children to "bake up" some clay treats.

2. Gingerbread is not just for holiday time! See page 72 for ideas to use a gingerbread theme as your "beginning of the year" unit.

3. Display a map or globe wherein you have labeled Germany, North America, and your locale by taping small strips of paper onto the globe. The globe will be used for the following geography activity. Show the cover of *The Gingerbread Boy* and share its title. Explain to the children that this story is a folk tale. Share that a folk tale is a special story that is told by parents to their children. Display the labeled globe. Ask them from what continent and/or large country they think the folk tale originated. (Note: Most people think it is from Europe [Germany], but it actually originated in North America [the United States].) Point to North America on the globe. If desired, mark it by taping a small paper gingerbread man (pattern, page 78) to the area. Read the story.

4. Make a child-size gingerbread boy from sturdy cardboard or wood by enlarging the pattern on pages 75–76. Attach a large clothespin or two to his chest with hot glue or epoxy glue. Decorate him using paints, markers, jewels, candy, etc. Position the gingerbread boy so that all can see him clearly. Use your cardboard guest to introduce activities, such as having him "hold" the literature book that will be read for the day, or hold a practice sheet that must be completed by the end of the school day, or hold a special treat for all to eat.

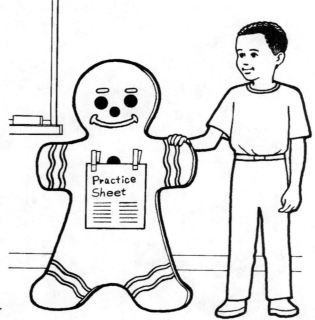

5. Make a pointer to use with the unit when doing chart work or reading big books. Simply make a gingerbread-man shape using the patterns on page 75–76. Decorate the shape and then glue it to the end of a 36" (91 cm) dowel or a children's baton. (The ones with glitter inside add a bit of sparkle.)

6. Display the gingerbread boy in the classroom. Ask children if they have ever seen or tasted a gingerbread cookie. (Recipe is on page 62.)

Overview of Activities *(cont.)*

Enjoying the Book

1. Read the book to the students and share the illustrations.

2. Make wall decorations to symbolize the running gingerbread boy. Each child will need to make a running silhouette, using his or her body outline. One at a time, unless you have extra assistance, have a child lie down in a running position (on his or her side) on an appropriate length of light-brown paper. Use a pencil to trace around the child's body. After he or she stands up, retrace the pencil line using a thick, black marker. Supply materials such as paint, markers, packing peanuts, fabric, etc., and have each child decorate his or her body shape. Display the running gingerbread children on the walls or in the hallway with a caption that reads, Catch Us If You Can!

3. Create a retelling-the-story game board (pages 11–12). Reproduce and cut out each page on the solid lines. Glue the two halves to the inside of a file folder to form the game board. Color the game board and laminate it, if desired. Use small, purchased gingerbread cookies for playing tokens or use small gingerbread-boy paper cutouts (pattern, page 78). You will also need to provide one die. The directions are on the game board.

4. Display modern-day farming equipment illustrations and/or photographs. Discuss the function of each machine. Explain to the children that when the gingerbread folk tale was first told, modern farming machines had not yet been invented. Tell them to look closely at the story's pictures to discover two types of workers that worked on wheat farms. Ask them to raise their hands when they see the workers (mowers and threshers). If possible, show the children some real wheat stalks and explain that it was a mower's job to cut the wheat with a tool called a sickle. It was a thresher's job to separate the wheat grains from the stalks of wheat by pounding them with a club against the ground. Now turn to the page that shows the woman placing raisins on the gingerbread boy. Share that the wheat that had been mowed and threshed had now been ground into flour for baking. Ask what the woman made (a cookie). Complete the sequencing activity found on page 15. Run one copy of page 15 for each child. Children color and cut apart pictures on the lines. Give each child one piece of 6" x 18" (15 cm x 46 cm) construction paper. Have children paste the pictures to the paper strip in the correct order.

Overview of Activities *(cont.)*

Enjoying the Book *(cont.)*

---

5. Go on a Gingerbread Boy Hunt! To create the hunt, read page 69. Pre-planning will be necessary, but the children will love the experience! If you made the child-size, cardboard gingerbread boy (page 6, Setting the Stage, #4), it will need to be removed from the room for this activity. Happy hunting!

6. Retell the *Gingerbread Boy* story, using the story strips on page 42. You will need a large pocket chart (or you can tape prepared strips to the chalkboard). You will also need a set of 3" x 5" (8 cm x 13 cm) index cards that each contain the name of a child in your class. You will need a second set of index cards with the words and/or pictures of these story characters: cow, horse, threshers, mowers, and a fox. To complete this activity, place the sentence strips in the correct order in the pocket chart. Place all cards in the pocket chart except the one marked with the star. The strip with the star is held and read five times.

As a class, read the sentences to see what is missing (the characters' names). Reread one sentence strip at a time and have the children tell you what character belongs in each sentence blank. Reread the entire story. Reread the story using the "star card" where approppriate. Remove the characters' cards and replace them with the first five name cards in the children's pre-made name cards pile. Repeat until all of the names have been used. After this activity, place the chart, the sentence strips, and the index cards in a center area for free-time use.

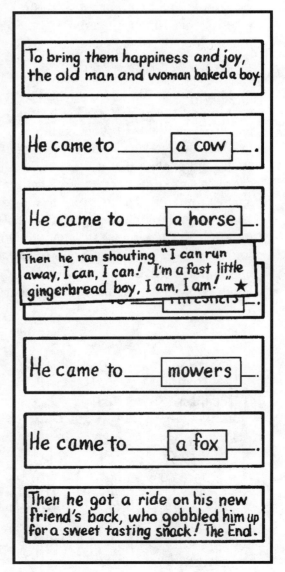

7. Teach the children "Run Away Song" on page 32. Make the Song Wheel (pages 13–14) by reproducing each page onto white construction paper, one set of the two pages per child. Allow the children to color the pictures and cut out the song wheels. Lay the gingerbread boy wheel on top of the character wheel and fasten the two wheels together, using a brad through the center holes. Sing the song again, using the wheel. Students should be able to view each character, at the appropriate time, through the wheel's window.

8. Combine the ingredients listed on page 58 to make a bottle of fun for the whole class to enjoy. This bottle is exciting, but can also have a calming effect on students.

9. Make gingerbread boy pop-up puppets. Follow the directions on page 56 to complete the puppets.

Overview of Activities *(cont.)*

Extending the Book

1. Children will love creating their own pop-up math pages (page 52). Write a different addition or subtraction problem on each of the smaller gingerbread boys. Have each child decorate the larger gingerbread boy and the background, using crayons, markers, or chalk. Cut out both gingerbread boys and attach them to the pre-made, pre-folded pop-up page. Show an example of a finished pop-up word problem. Have each child write out his or her own mathematical story problem (text) to match the problem written on his or her smaller gingerbread boy. Have the child glue the larger gingerbread boy to the actual pop-up section. The smaller gingerbread boy will be placed next to the word problem. Display the pages separately. Later, if desired, place them into a class book by combining the pages, being careful to arrange them so that the gingerbread boys still pop-up. Finally, add a cover.

2. Play a game of "Who Stole the Cookie from the Cookie Jar?" with the students. Seat the children on the floor in a large circle. Make a gingerbread person from paper or craft foam (pattern, page 78). Place him in a medium-size glass or actual cookie jar in the middle of the circle. Choose one child to cover his or her eyes. After that child has closed his or her eyes, point to a child in the circle to come to the center, quietly take the gingerbread-boy cookie from the cookie jar, return to his or her place in the circle, and sit down on top of the gingerbread boy. The child whose eyes were closed is now to open them and try to guess who is hiding the cookie. The child gets a total of four guesses. If he or she is successful, another turn is earned. However, if the child is unable to guess where the cookie is hidden, the child hiding the cookie becomes the new sleuth. A variation is to place the cookie or glass jar on a tabletop and ask the children to hide their eyes. Choose one child to come up and hide the cookie somewhere in the room. When the rest of the class begins the guessing process, encourage them to ask questions that need yes or no responses.

3. What a fox! Children will love making the story's villain using the Japanese art of origami. Follow the directions on page 60.

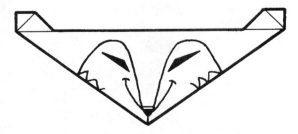

Overview of Activities *(cont.)*

Extending the Book *(cont.)*

---

4. Share some background information on ginger (Gingerlinks, page 67). If possible, show your children an actual ginger root as well as a container of powdered ginger, a spice available at most grocery stores. Explain that ginger, a spice, starts as a small seed. When the seed grows into a plant, the roots are harvested (show the root). Explain that the root is sometimes ground into a fine powder.

5. Complete a scent-sational activity, It Just Makes Scents, on page 47. To prepare for this activity, reproduce the gingerbread boy onto cardstock for each child. Have the children color each gingerbread boy brown. Then have them spread a small amount of white glue onto each gingerbread boy's tummy. Have an adult, or the child, sprinkle one of the four spices listed onto the glue on each gingerbread boy. Tap off any excess; allow the glue to dry. (Extension: Each child can make a spice book. The book's covers can be made using two 6" (15 cm) brown (or colored brown) paper plates. Cut apart the completed four scented rectangles. Place these pages in between the plates so that the left-side edge of the plates is even. Punch two holes through all the layers. Bind the book together using two 4" (10 cm) pieces of yarn or string. Have the children create gingerbread faces on the front covers of their books, using crayons, markers, glitter, yarn, etc.)

6. Read other versions of *The Gingerbread Boy* (Bibliography, page 80). Compare the similarities and differences between the tales. Enlarge the Venn diagram (page 16) onto tagboard and laminate. Use a dry-erase marker to record children's responses. Use a small piece of felt to erase the children's responses on the Venn diagram.

7. Review with the children where *The Gingerbread Boy* originated (North America). Share that the North American people are alike in some ways, but different in others. Have the children brainstorm and give examples of ways they are alike and different (list their suggestions on the chalkboard or chart paper).

8. Sing the "alphabet" song to review the order of the letters of the alphabet. Have the children complete the adorable Gingerbread Boy Cookie dot-to-dot activity on page 44.

9. Give each child a copy of the gingerbread-boy pattern (page 74) reproduced on tagboard. Establish that the gingerbread boy outlines all look the same. Challenge them to make them look different! Using a variety of craft materials, have the children decorate their patterns. When all of the "gingerbread kids" are done, punch a hole near the tip of each kid's hands. Loop a 5" (13 cm) piece of ribbon or yarn through two different kids' hands and tie it in a bow. Repeat the process with all the gingerbread kids to create a garland. Hang it up for all to see and enjoy.

File Folder Game Board

Directions

1. Roll the die and move the required number of spaces.
2. Describe what is happening in the story as you pass or land on a picture.

File Folder Game Board *(cont.)*

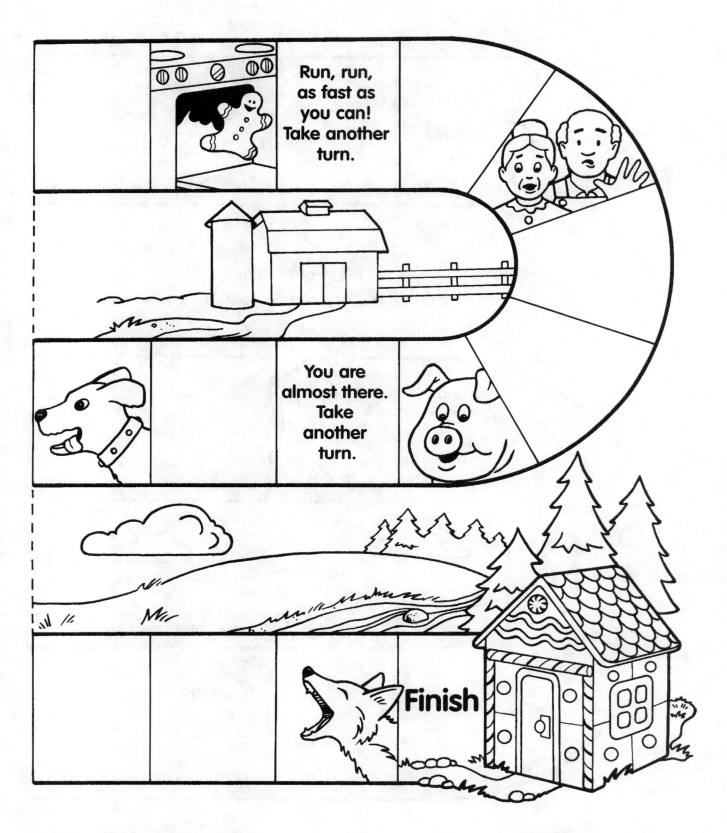

12

Song Wheel

Directions: Cut out the wheels on pages 13 and 14. Color them. Place The Gingerbread Boy wheel on top of the wheel with the story characters. Connect the two wheels using a brad.

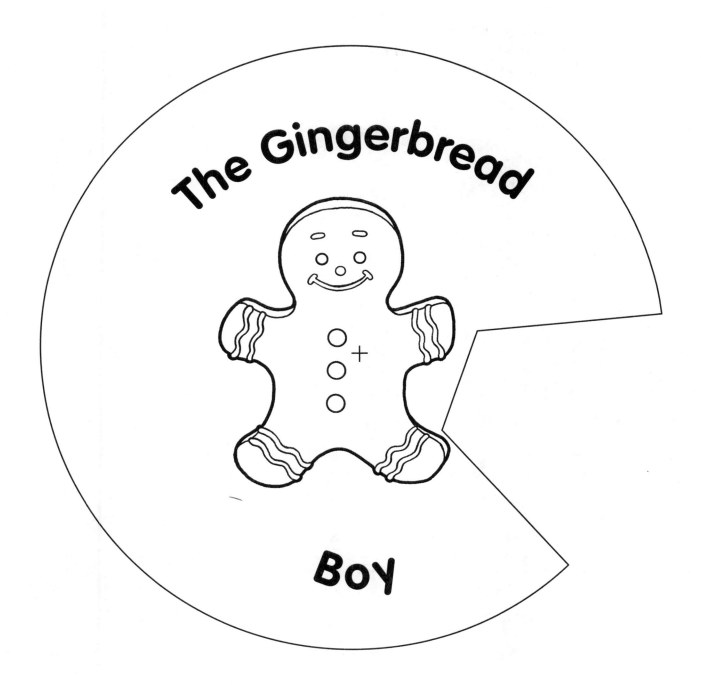

Song Wheel *(cont.)*

Directions: Cut out the wheels on pages 13 and 14. Color and laminate them. Place The Gingerbread Boy wheel on top of the wheel with the story characters. Connect the two wheels using a brad.

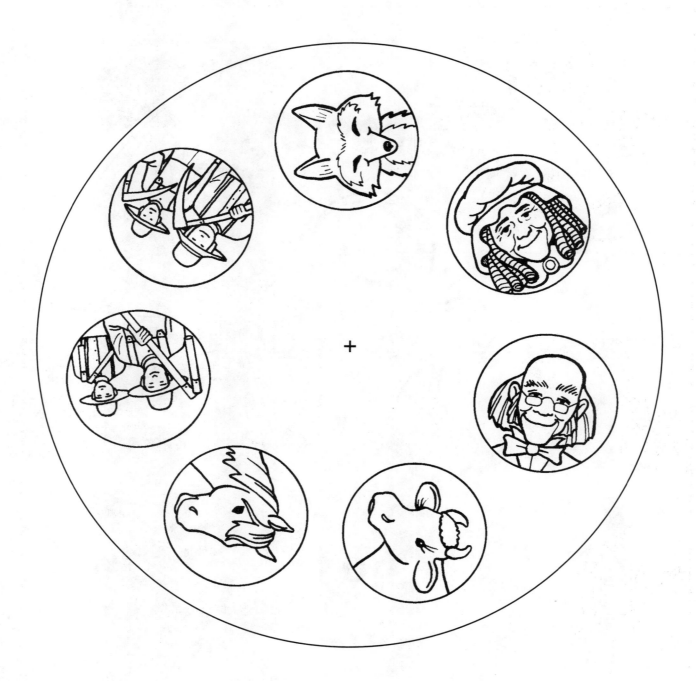

Making a Gingerbread Boy

Directions: Color the pictures and cut them apart on the dotted lines. Glue or paste the pictures onto a 6" x 18" strip of paper in the correct order. Begin with the first step in making a gingerbread boy.

Venn Diagram

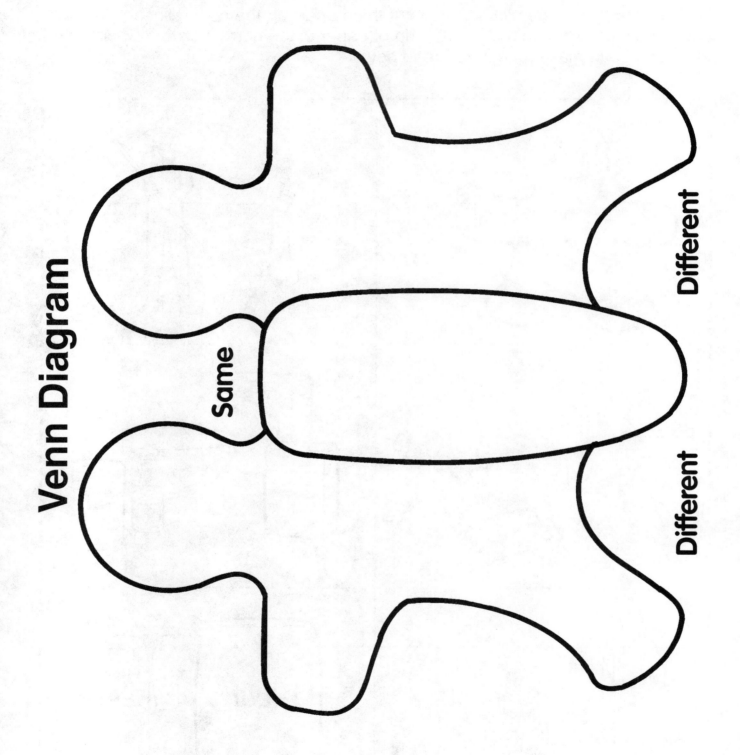

Venn Diagram

Same

Different

Different

Character Cards

Directions: Color and cut out the cards.

little old woman

little old man

gingerbread boy

cow

horse

threshers

mowers

fox

Gingerbread Baby

by Jan Brett

Summary

Gingerbread Baby *is a delicious twist to the traditional nursery story* The Gingerbread Boy. *The sassy Gingerbread Baby is born when Matti opens the oven door too soon. He runs through the snowbound Swiss village teasing everyone in his path. However, Matti does not join in the race to catch the Gingerbread Baby. Rather, he creates a gingerbread house in which to entice the baby to come back home.*

The outline below is a suggested plan for using various activities that are presented in this unit.

Sample Plan

Lesson 1

- Review *The Gingerbread Boy* (page 19, Enjoying the Book, #2).
- Read *Gingerbread Baby* to the class.
- Act out the story using the puppets on pages 22–25.
- Complete a character word search activity (page 30).
- Send home the activity letter to encourage family fun (page 73).

Lesson 2

- Introduce a bell-ringer activity (page 21).
- Reread *Gingerbread Baby*.
- Retell the story focusing on story sequence.
- Use the puppet props (page 19, #4).
- Teach the "Run Away Song" (page 32).
- Complete the maze activity (page 27).

Lesson 3

- Try a new bell-ringer activity (page 21).
- Sing "Run Away Song" (page 32).
- Review the story, focusing on how the Gingerbread Baby came to be.
- Work on telling time (page 20, #4).
- Discuss following a recipe, then make a recipe (pages 62–64).
- Complete the time worksheet, the Cookies Are Ready (page 49).

Lesson 4

- Introduce a new bell-ringer activity (page 21).
- Sing "Run Away Song" (page 32).
- Discuss homes (page 20, #3).
- Complete the graphing activity (page 53).
- Play a game (page 31).
- Enjoy a "surprising" activity (page 20, #10).

Overview of Activities

Setting the Stage

1. Create a gingerbread house, using one large, empty box (e.g., oven, refrigerator, or television). Paint the outside of the box brown or cover it with brown paper. Make a front door and side windows by cutting through the paper and cardboard, using a box cutter. Decorate the box with paint, fabric, glitter, etc. If desired, add candy canes made by painting paper towel tubes with red and white stripes.

2. Create the "Our Gingerbread Village" bulletin board (page 71). Send home copies of the Family Fun letter (page 73) and be sure to include the date by which you need the project returned.

Enjoying the Book

1. Children will love making their own Gingerbread Baby pop-up puppets! Just follow the directions on page 56 to create a crafty little guy who's popping out of the oven.

2. Briefly review *The Gingerbread Boy* by asking the following questions:

   * Who made the Gingerbread Boy?
   * Who chased the Gingerbread Boy?
   * What was the weather like in the story?

   Now show the cover and read the title of *Gingerbread Baby*. Just by comparing the covers and the first pages of the two stories, ask the children how the stories are different.

3. Help the Gingerbread Baby escape the parade of anxious characters by leading him to Matti's gingerbread house. Have the children complete the maze activity, Catch Me If You Can!, on page 27.
   Variation: This worksheet might also be used for a sequencing review of the story, done as a large-group activity.

4. Have the children use stick puppets to retell the story. Run one copy of pages 22–25 on white construction paper or tagboard. Color and cut out each character. Attach each cutout by stapling or pasting it to a tongue depressor or craft stick. If desired, use the cutouts on a flannel board. Glue flannel or felt to the back of each prepared character.

5. Play a new twist to "Doggie, Doggie, Where's Your Bone?" This time say, "Matti, Matti, Where's Your Home?" See page 31 for the game's directions.

6. Children will enjoy acting out the story while using the gingerbread house prop (see above, Setting the Stage, # 1). Perhaps, if time allows, students could create paper-plate masks to wear during their performances.

7. Find them if you can! Children will have fun looking for the story's characters in the word search on page 30.

8. Teach the children "Run Away Song" (page 32).

9. Introduce the Bell-Ringer Activities (page 21). These special activities can be used at any time to enhance a teaching moment or generate discussion.

Overview of Activities

Enjoying the Book *(cont.)*

10. Surprise your children with this fun activity! Make one small gingerbread figure, using the patterns on page 74, for each child. Before school or while the children are out of the room, place the gingerbread figure inside each child's prepared gingerbread house (page 77). Write the following note on the chalkboard or chart paper to lead the children to where they will find their surprise!

I ran away from the cat and dog,
But now I'm slowing down.
I need a place to rest my feet
From all the running around.
The door to your little house was open,
So I made myself at home.
Please don't be mad at me,
I've just been waiting for you to come!

Extending the Book

1. Review or teach the process of computing simple subtraction story problems using the Math Story Work Mat on pages 28 and 29. Run several copies of pages 28 and 29. Color, cut, and paste the pages together to create one scene, and laminate it. Supply children with small snack cups filled with counters (raisins or cinnamon candies) for solving math problems. For example, "The Gingerbread Baby put five raisins by the cat. The cat ate three. How many are left?" When students finish the activity, allow them to eat their treats.

2. For a spatial relationship lesson, provide each child with a small gingerbread cookie and ask him or her to follow oral directions. For example, "Put the Gingerbread Baby under the goat."

3. Discuss "homes" with the children—characteristics, similarities, differences, who lives in them, etc. Have a "show-and-tell" time allowing them to show their family fun gingerbread box houses (page 73).

4. Teach the concept of telling time by the hour, half-hour, etc. Run 10–12 copies of page 26 on light brown construction paper. Fill in the clock numbers and desired time in the Gingerbread Baby's belly, using a permanent marker. Using the oven-door piece, make a matching time written in digital time. Laminate all the pieces, if desired. Use this as a large-group matching activity. Then place the materials in a math learning center area for additional practice. During class time or for an at-home assignment, complete The Cookies Are Ready worksheet (page 49).

5. Have the children complete the graphing activity (page 53).

6. Follow the directions on page 46 to create a winter crystal garden for your classroom. Add a store-bought gingerbread cookie to the finished garden to simulate Gingerbread Baby running through the snowbound village.

Classroom Activities

Bell-Ringer Activities

Choose one of the following activities to introduce a new concept, review a previous lesson, or to simply get the children thinking. These are ideal for daily journal writing as well.

1. Matti opened the oven door too soon and out jumped the Gingerbread Baby. What would have happened if Matti had left the cookie in the oven too long?

2. Choose a sentence from the story and write it on the board, changing its punctuation, word spellings, and/or capitalization. Have children rewrite the sentence, making all the necessary corrections. This may be done as a daily activity.

3. Have children list as many of the characters chasing Gingerbread Baby as they can remember. You may wish to ask them to do this alphabetically.

4. Ask children to write a sentence telling how Matti caught Gingerbread Baby. If time allows, have them illustrate their sentences.

5. Ask the children how *Gingerbread Baby* ended differently from *The Gingerbread Boy*.

6. Have the children describe Matti's clothing.

Estimation Ideas

Place a small desk at a convenient spot in the classroom. Supply pencils, sticky notes, a name chart, and one of the ideas listed below (change daily). Children may write their estimations on sticky notes and post them on the name chart as they come in each morning. At some point during the day, find the answer to the problem together. This is a great way to take attendance too!

1. Fill a small jar with candies (e.g., gum drops, chocolate chips, gummy bears). Have the children guess how many there are.

2. Display an empty frozen-juice can and one candy stick. Have the children estimate how many candy sticks it would take to fill the can.

3. Place graham crackers in a small clear sandwich bag and have the children guess how many squares of crackers there are inside.

4. Have the children estimate how many teddy-bear crackers are in a small box or tin.

5. Set out a small bowl and two to three pieces of one type of cereal. Ask the children to guess how many pieces of cereal it would take to fill the bowl.

6. Have children estimate how many sticks of gum would fill a matchbox.

Puppet Props

22

Puppet Props *(cont.)*

Puppet Props *(cont.)*

Puppet Props *(cont.)*

Is It Time Yet?

26

Catch Me If You Can!

Math Story Work Mat

Directions: Connect pages 28 and 29 at the dotted line. See page 20, #1 for directions.

Math Story Work Mat *(cont.)*

Find Me If You Can

Directions: Find each word from the list in the puzzle below and circle it. Figure out the mystery word, circle it, and then write it.

```
s   c   m   a   r   t   h   a   g
g   a   a   k   l   a   f   o   x
o   d   d   i   d   m   o   m   o
a   d   e   a   p   y   q   h   f
t   y   l   t   m   a   t   t   i
s   i   i   t   i   a   c   a   o
r   t   n   c   l   e   r   s   u
b   d   e   a   k   y   m   h   r
a   a   y   t   m   u   d   o   g
b   d   m   z   a   h   o   r   d
y   m   a   f   n   x   a   s   p
d   b   p   i   g   o   i   c   e
```

Mystery word clue:

What did Gingerbread Baby jump on to cross the river? _____

Find and circle your answer.

Word Bank			
baby	fox	Matti	dad
cat	goats	milkman	Martha
dog	Madeline	mom	pig

Matti, Matti, Where's Your Home?

Teacher Preparation

Make a gingerbread baby and a gingerbread house from laminated construction paper or felt, using one of the patterns on pages 74 and 77. This is a twist on the game "Doggie, Doggie, Where's Your Bone?"

Directions

1. Seat the children on the floor, all facing the same direction.

2. Choose one child to come to the front and stand him or her with his or her back to the rest of the class. This child holds the gingerbread baby.

3. Hand the house to one of the children sitting in the group. This child will sit on the house to hide it from the chosen student.

4. Have the group of children call out, "Matti, Matti, where's your home?"

5. The child holding the gingerbread baby turns around and tries to guess (three guesses) the child who is hiding the home. If he or she successfully guesses the person holding the house, he or she has earned another turn. However, if the guesses are unsuccessful, the child holding the house comes forward to become the new gingerbread baby.

Gingerbread Baby Songs

Run Away Song

(Sung to the tune of "99 Bottles of Pop on the Wall")

I am the Gingerbread Baby

And I'm happy as can be.

I jumped out of the oven

And now no one can catch me!

Oh! I ran away from Matti's mom

Away from his father too.

Away from the cat, away from the dog,

Away from the goats I flew!

I ran away from Martha,

Away from Madeline too.

Away from the pig, away from the fox,

Away from the milkman too!

Oh! I am the Gingerbread Baby

And happy as can be.

Matti made a gingerbread house

Especially for me!

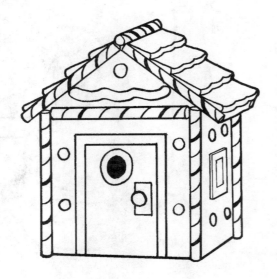

The House

(Sung to the tune of "Twinkle, Twinkle Little Star")

Gingerbread Baby come and see

The house I made for you from me.

It is sweet and colored bright,

It will keep you safe at night.

Gingerbread Baby come and see

The house I made for you from me.

32

Let's Make a Gingerbread House

by Daphne Ransom

Summary

Let's Make A Gingerbread House *is a mini-book designed to allow the children to make their own gingerbread houses. This following-directions book shares a little bit of the history of gingerbread houses, then leads the students through the steps to make a simple gingerbread house using graham crackers. An added plus—the text is written in a rhyming format, which makes the instructions fun and easy to remember.*

The outline below is a suggested plan for using various activities that are presented in this unit.

Sample Plan

Lesson 1

- Choose one of the estimation activities (page 21).
- Introduce the mini-book (page 34, Enjoying the Book, #1).
- Do one of the phonemic activities (page 45).
- Complete Sweet Words (page 34, Enjoying the Book, #2).
- Review colors and shapes (page 35, #2).

Lesson 2

- Do an estimation activity (page 21).
- Reread the mini-book (page 34, Enjoying the Book, #3).
- Choose a phonemic activity (page 45).
- Sing "A Gingerbread House" (page 61).
- Complete a mini-book (page 34, Setting the Stage, #3).

Lesson 3

- Do an estimation activity (page 21).
- Reread the mini-book (page 34, Enjoying the Book, #3).
- Choose one of the phonemic activities (page 45).
- Complete the rhyming activity (page 35, Extending the Book, #4).
- Create a Big Book (page 34, Enjoying the Book, #4).

Lesson 4

- Choose one of the estimation activities (page 21).
- Teach or review simple addition facts (page 35, #3).
- Complete the Candy Counting worksheet (page 51).
- Reread the mini-book.
- Sing "A Gingerbread House" (page 61).
- Choose one of the culminating activities (pages 69–70).

Overview of Activities

Setting the Stage

1. Set out a number of assorted candies and graham crackers along with small containers or an empty egg carton for a sorting activity. Encourage children to use color, size, and shape in their sorting efforts.

2. Create a big-book version of the mini-book (pages 36–40). Enlarge the pages to the desired size and color them. Cut out and assemble the book in the correct order.

3. Reproduce a mini-book (pages 36–40) for each child. Cut out the pages, assemble in sequential order, and staple them together along the left-side edge to form the mini-book. (Note: Children can color the books themselves as a planned or fun-time activity.)

Enjoying the Book

1. Introduce the mini-book (page 34, Setting the Stage, #3). Explain that this book is not a "story" book, rather, it is an "instructional" book—a book that tells you how to do something—make a gingerbread house. Read the mini-book one page at a time, asking the children to listen carefully for the things that are needed to make a gingerbread house. When finished, ask them to recall the ingredients needed and list them on chart paper.

2. Have the children complete Sweet Words (page 43) by filling in the blanks with the appropriate letters in order to complete the spelling of many different confections. This will also give them some ideas of what they may wish to use in later lessons when making their own gingerbread houses.

3. Reread the mini-book together. Focus on the rhyming words. Explain that when words rhyme, they have the same ending sound. The beginning sound is what changes (give some verbal examples such as, sea-Germany, know-go, treat-neat). Have them come up with their own rhyming words.

4. Create a Big Book for your classroom library. Cut two large house shapes (page 77) from cardboard or tagboard. Enlarge the pattern. These will be the covers. Allow the children to help decorate the front cover. Give each child a 12" x 18" (30 cm x 46 cm) piece of white paper. Ask them to write (or pre-write), "I'd like to live in a gingerbread house because . . . " Have them verbally dictate or write their responses and illustrate them accordingly. Put the book together by placing the children's pages between the covers. Punch holes at even intervals along the left side and bind the pages with book rings or by tying 6" (15 cm) pieces of yarn.

5. Review where the first gingerbread person was made (North America) and mark it on a classroom map or globe using a paper gingerbread person. After reading the gingerbread house mini-book, find where the first gingerbread was made (Germany) and mark it using a small paper house shape. Follow up the research with the Origin of Gingerbread worksheet on page 54. Children can cut out the pictures at the bottom of the page, paste them on the correct areas of the map, and then color the pictures. Children then fill in the blanks to complete the sentence.

34

Overview of Activities *(cont.)*

Extending the Book

1. Read the story *Hansel and Gretel* (Bibliography, page 80). Discuss the materials used to make the house in this folk tale. Show the children the gingerbread house in *Gingerbread Baby* and *Hansel and Gretel.* Have them compare how they are alike and how they are different.

2. Review shapes and colors with Yummy Shapes (page 48). Have children use the color/shape code to complete the activity.

3. Review the concept of simple addition before assigning page 51. Try hands-on practice using teddy-bear shaped graham crackers or animal crackers to reinforce addition skills while completing the worksheet.

4. Create a rhyming learning center by making eight to ten copies of pages 75 and 76. Color both parts of the gingerbread boy and cut them out. Glue on pictures of rhyming objects to both the top and the bottom parts. Children will enjoy this challenging activity of matching the rhyming pictures.

5. Children love jump-rope rhymes! Get a jump rope and choose one of the rhymes on page 66. Practicing this activity will strengthen children's coordination and make recess time more fun!

6. Enhance children's fine-motor skills by creating sewing cards. Run copies of page 77 on tagboard or construction paper. Color them and laminate them. Punch holes at even intervals around the house design. Supply white yarn or a shoelace and demonstrate how to thread the shoelace around the house to decorate it.

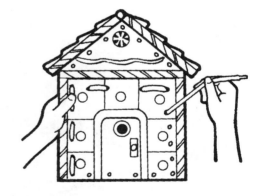

7. Help the children learn their addresses by attaching an addressed label to each of their milk carton gingerbread houses (page 72). Review these addresses, one-on-one, three to four times a week. Variation: Run one copy of the Gingerbread House Pattern (page 77) for each child to color and cut out. Add their addresses to the roof and display them.

8. Children will enjoy making a gingerbread man holding an American flag or creating a gingerbread house with a German flag after reviewing the origins of both (page 34, Enjoying the Book, #5). Run copies of the Large Gingerbread Boy Pattern on pages 75–76 and the Gingerbread House Pattern (page 77). Also run copies of the flags (page 55). Place them in an appropriate center. Have actual copies or pictures of the flags on display. Have children color and cut out all the pieces. Glue a straw to the left side of each flag and attach the flags to the pattern pieces by gluing or stapling.

9. If you have access to the Internet in your classroom, have the children check out Gingerlinks (page 67). Then they can complete Gingerbread Facts (page 68).

Gingerbread House Mini-book

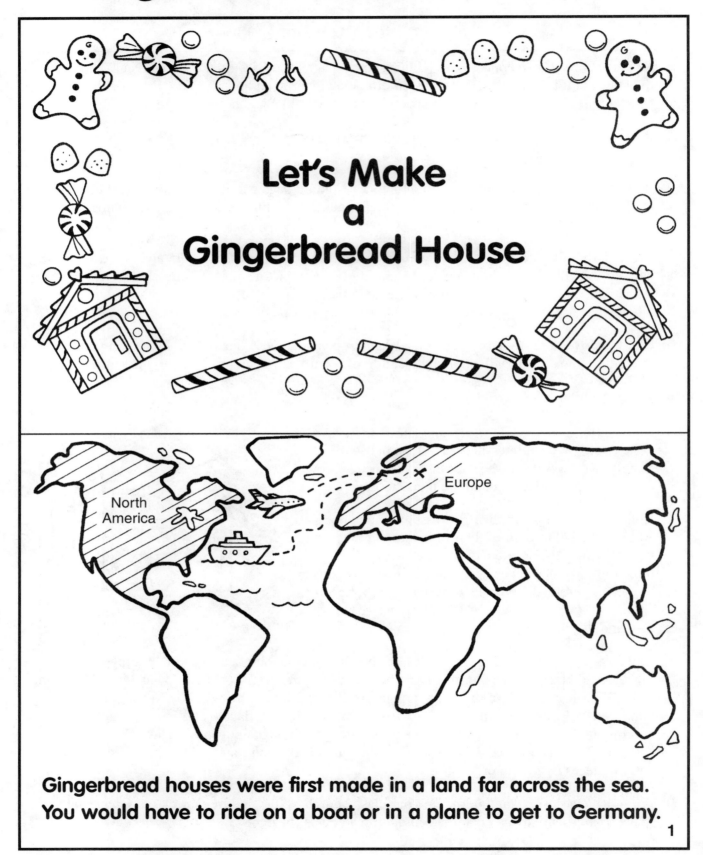

Let's Make a Gingerbread House

Gingerbread houses were first made in a land far across the sea. You would have to ride on a boat or in a plane to get to Germany.

1

Gingerbread House Mini-book *(cont.)*

This tasty treat is called Lubkuchenhaus, you know.
Let's make one now, just like they did many years ago.

2

With frosting and crackers, we'll make this tasty treat.
Just follow these directions—be careful and be neat!

3

Gingerbread House Mini-book *(cont.)*

You need eight squares of graham crackers, and frosting from a can.
Lots of yummy candies and other sweet goodies in a pan.

4

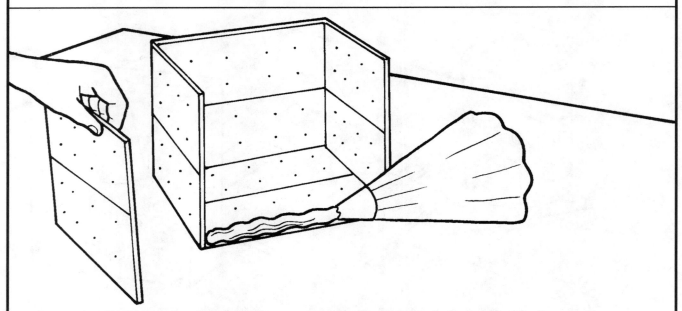

You'll need one cracker for the floor—place frosting around its four side edges.

Take four more crackers and stand them up for walls—now make some roof wedges.

5

Gingerbread House Mini-book *(cont.)*

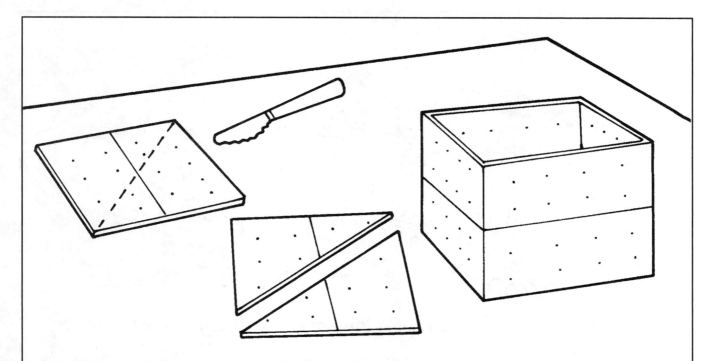

Take another square and cut it diagonally in two.
You will have two triangles, now here is what to do.

6

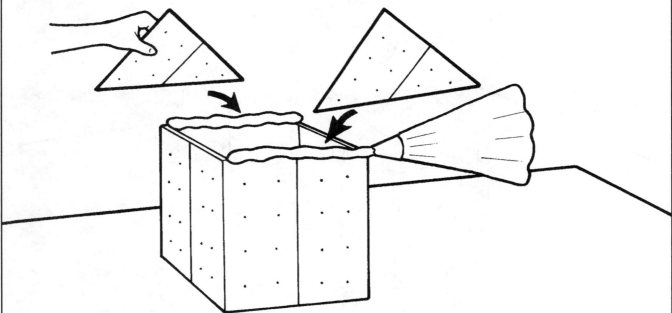

Put frosting along the top edge of the end walls.
Place the triangles on the frosting—hold in place so neither
triangle falls.

7

Gingerbread House Mini-book *(cont.)*

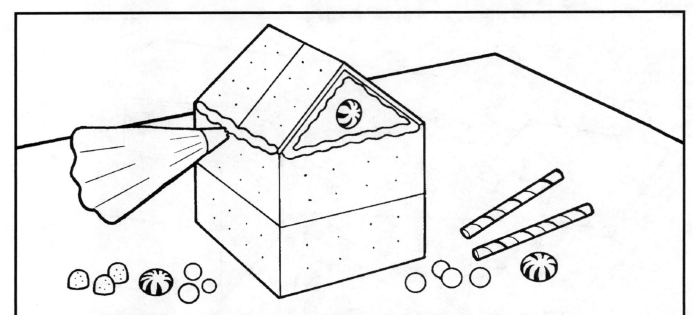

Place frosting on all the roof edges and lay down the last two squares.

Now all you need to do is decorate your house—maybe you'll make some stairs.

8

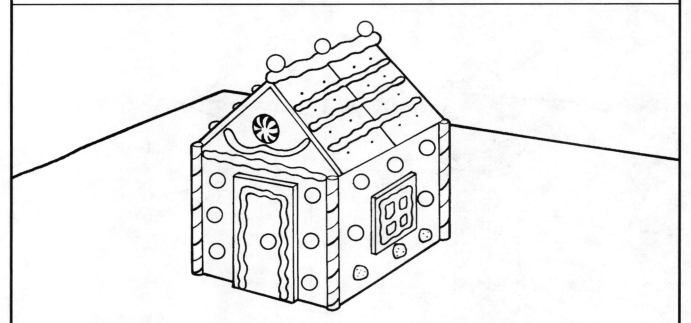

Dab frosting here and frosting there—add the candies that you like.

You're finished now, let's eat it up with Jimmy, Sue, and Mike!

9

Sweet Poetry

Never Eat Candy in Bed

"Never eat candy in bed"
Is what my mother said.
It will stick to your hair and your underwear
And stick to your toes and the end of your nose.
The cat's tail will be stuck to your pillow.
The dog's ears will be stuck to your quilt.
Your teeth will get soft like a marshmallow,
And false ones will have to be built.
So . . .
Remember what my mother said,
"Never eat candy in bed!"

Making Gingerbread

Gingerbread is made from flour and sugar,
Cinnamon, molasses, cloves, and ginger.
Add some eggs and stir real well.
Make some for home and some to sell.
Roll out the dough and cut out the men,
Decorate with raisins, and pop in the oven.

Soft and Gooey

A gingerbread boy is quite a sight,
He's soft, he's brown, he's gooey.
He smiles, he winks, he jumps, he runs,
Quick, gobble him up, he's chewy.

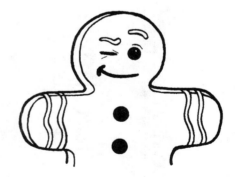

Anytime! Anywhere!
(*Clapping Game*)

Gingerbread is great for any time of day,   *Hands slap lap, clap, right hands together, clap.*
Yesterday, tomorrow, or even today.   *Hands slap lap, clap, left hands together, clap.*
Eat it when it's warm. Eat it when it's cool.   *Hands slap lap, clap, right hands together, clap,*
Eat it at Grandma's, or eat it at school!   *Hands slap lap, clap, both hands hit at the same time, clap.*

Directions: Have children pair up and sit facing each other. Explain that they will be alternating clapping their right and left hands together and tapping their laps as they say the poem.

Story Strips

Directions: Make five of strip 1. Make one of strips 2–4. Strip 3 is the repetitive-text strip. Hold Strip 3 over each sentence strip after the text has been read (except the last strip) and read the repetitive text.

1. He came to _____ .

2. To bring them happiness and joy, the old woman and old man baked a boy.

3. Then he ran shouting, "I can run away, I can, I can! I'm a fast little gingerbread boy, I am, I am!" ★

4. Then, he got a ride on his new friend's back, who gobbled him up for a sweet tasting snack! The End.

Sweet Words

Directions: Use the word bank to fill in the blanks.

___ u ___   ___ r ___ ___s

___ ___ p ___ ___ ___ m ___ ___ t

___ h ___ ___ o ___ ___ ___   c ___ ___ p ___

___ r ___ ___ ___ e ___ ___

c ___ ___ ___ a ___ ___ ___ ___

___ ___ m   ___ a ___ ___ s

___ ___ r ___ h ___ ___ ___ ___ ___ ___ w ___

___ ___ n ___ ___   ___ ___ i c ___ ___

___ ___ ___ s ___ ___ s

___ ___ ___ ___ e ___ ___ ___ d   ___ ___ e ___ ___

___ ___ ___ a r ___ ___ ___ ___ s

Word Bank

peppermint	pretzels	chocolate chips
marshmallows	shredded wheat	spearmints
raisins	candy sticks	gum drops
cinnamons	gum balls	

Gingerbread Boy Cookie

Directions: Connect the dots. Color.

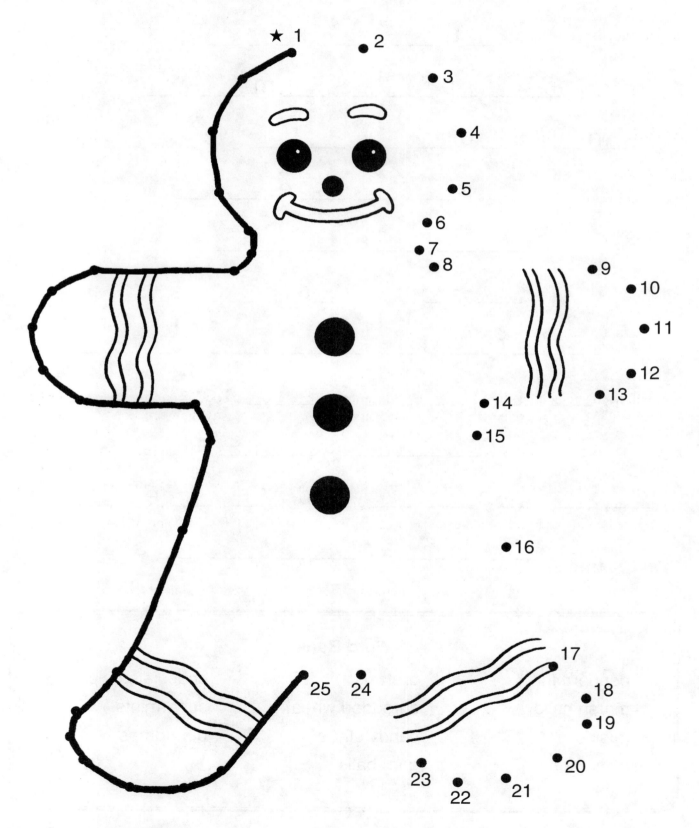

Phonemic Activities

Syllabication Activity

Have the children clap or jump out the syllables of the names of several types of candies (e.g., cinnamons, peppermint, wintergreen).

mint
1

gum—drop
1 + 1

win—ter—green
1 + 1 + 1

Syllabication Activity

Children find the parts to words as they touch their bodies from their heads (syllable) to their toes (5 syllables).

Each body part touched equals one syllable.

head—1   fox

head/shoulders—2   ba—by

head/shoulders/waist—3   cin—na—mon

head/shoulders/waist/knees—4   gin—ger—bread—boy

head/shoulders/waist/knees/toes—5   pep—per—mint—can—dies

Syllabication Activity

You will need sticky notes for this activity. Place the same number of sticky notes on the board or flat surface you are using as there are in the word you are going to study. Say the word slowly and touch each sticky note as a part of the word is said. Do not write the words on the paper. Then ask a child to remove the sticky note that represents a particular part of a word. (i.e., Place three sticky notes on the board. Say "peppermint" slowly while pointing to the first sticky note when you say "*pep*," the second sticky note when you say "*per*," and the third sticky note when you say "*mint*." Do the same when the children repeat the word. Now ask one child to come forward and remove the sticky note that represented "mint".) Repeat the process but use different numbers of syllables and different words.

What Sound Is Missing?

Give the children a "sweet" word and ask them to repeat it. Focus on the sound of the word. Then say the word again, omitting the initial consonant. Ask the children, "What sound is missing?"
(For example, say "mint." Now say "int." "What sound is missing?")

Let's Try Sound Substitution!

Have the children repeat a "tasty" word after you, such as "marshmallow." Now ask them to change the /m/ sound at the beginning to a /t/ sound. They'll have fun making these silly words.

marshmallow—tarshmallow   cracker—tacker
icing—ticing   candy—tandy

A Winter Crystal Garden

A crystal garden is a garden created through chemical reactions. It can be beautiful to look at. When your crystals begin to grow, leave the garden in a place where everyone can see it.

Materials

- 3 charcoal briquettes
- ³/₄ cup (180 mL) water
- ¹/₄ cup (60 mL) laundry bluing
- ¹/₄ cup (60 mL) salt
- 1 tablespoon (15 mL) ammonia

- 1 glass bowl
- 1 mixing bowl
- food coloring
- store-bought gingerbread cookie or teddy-bear-shaped graham cracker

Directions for Students

(with adult supervision)

1. Place the briquettes in a glass bowl.
2. Pour the food coloring on the briquettes.
3. Carefully mix the other ingredients together. Pour the mixture over the briquettes. Crystals will form in a few days.
4. Place the gingerbread cookie in the garden.

Draw your crystal garden below.

It Just Makes Scents

Directions: Color each gingerbread boy brown. Spread glue on each stomach. Add the spice suggested.

ginger

cinnamon

nutmeg

allspice

Yummy Shapes

Directions: Color the gingerbread house, using the color/shape code shown below to complete the activity. Fill in the remaining spaces with brown.

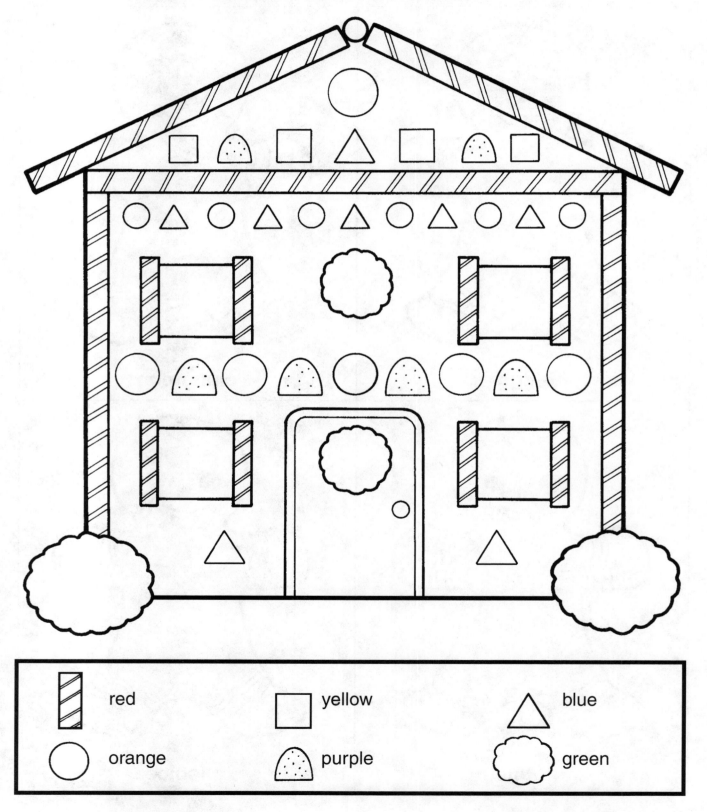

	red		yellow		blue
	orange		purple		green

The Cookies Are Ready

Directions: Draw a line matching the times on the Gingerbread Baby's tummy to the same digital time shown on the oven door.

How Many Cookies?

Mom made 8 cookies. Sue ate 3.

How many cookies were left? _____

Pam baked 10 cookies. Ned took 4.

How many cookies did Pam have left? _____

Sid had 6 cookies. He gave 1 to Dan.

How many cookies did Sid have left? _____

Nan made 9 cookies. She ate 2.

How many cookies did she have left? _____

Candy Counting

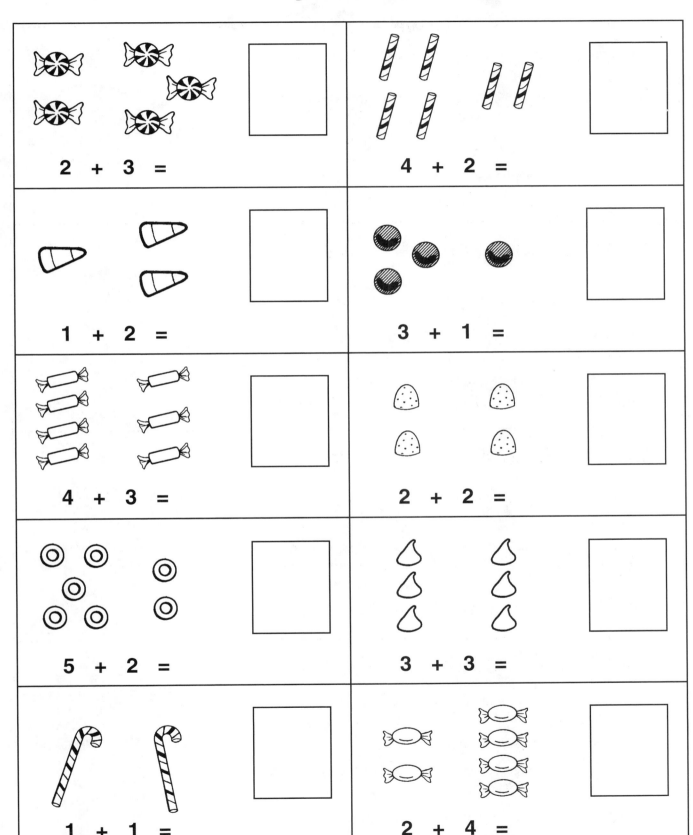

2 + 3 =

4 + 2 =

1 + 2 =

3 + 1 =

4 + 3 =

2 + 2 =

5 + 2 =

3 + 3 =

1 + 1 =

2 + 4 =

Gingerbread Boy Math Pop-up Page

Materials

- 8 ½" x 11" (21.5 cm x 28 cm) piece of construction paper
- markers
- scissors
- copies of large and small gingerbread boys, page 78

Teacher Preparation

1. Cut out the small gingerbread boys and write a different subtraction problem on each one before handing them out.

2. Prepare pop-up pages for students, using the directions below.

Directions for the Pop-up Page Preparation

1. Fold the construction paper in half (hamburger style). In the middle of the folded edge, mark two dots 1" (2.54 cm) apart.

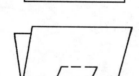

2. Starting at the dots, draw two lines, each 2" (5 cm) long, towards the opposite edge of the paper (away from the fold.) Cut on these lines, starting from the folded edge.

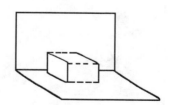

3. Fold the cut strip back and fold it forward again to form creases. Open the paper and hold it like a tent. Push the cut strip through to the other side of your paper. Close the paper and press firmly. Open to see the pop-up strip.

Directions to Students

1. Look at the math problem on the small gingerbread boy. Write a story problem that goes with the number problem on the pop-up card.

2. Color and cut out the large gingerbread boy.

3. Glue the smaller gingerbread boy next to your story problem on the card.

4. Attach the larger gingerbread boy to the pop-up strip.

Candy Graph

Directions: Color the gingerbread house. Color each type of candy on the house a different color. For example, make all the canes red.

Graph

Color one block for each candy used on the gingerbread house.

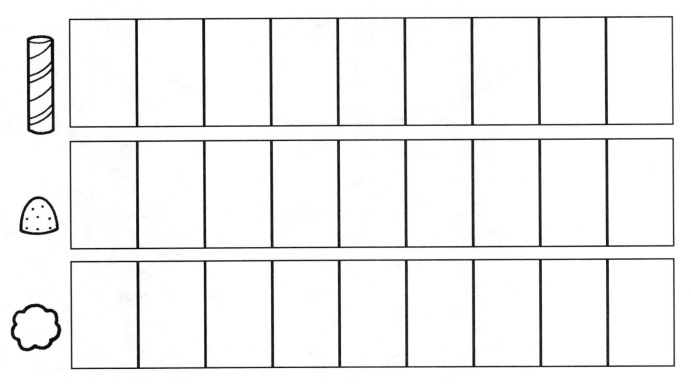

Origin of Gingerbread

The gingerbread boy was first made in _____.

The very first gingerbread house was created in _____.

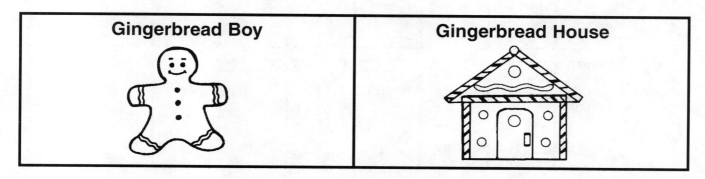

Gingerbread Boy	Gingerbread House

American and German Flags

Directions: Color and cut out the flags. Attach a straw to the left side of each flag.

Black

Red

Gold

Gingerbread Art

Pop-up Puppet
Materials
- small milk cartons (one per child)
- contact paper
- tongue depressors or craft sticks (one per child)
- Gingerbread Baby pattern (page 74) or Gingerbread Boy patterns (page 75–76)
- white construction paper
- crayons, scissors
- utility knife
- black permanent marker
- glue or a stapler

Teacher Preparation
1. Wash the small milk cartons and cut off the folded tops.
2. Cover the cartons with contact paper.
3. Using a utility knife, make a slit in the bottom of each carton large enough for a tongue depressor or craft stick to slide through.
4. Make one copy of a gingerbread baby or a gingerbread boy on white construction paper for each child.

Directions to Students
1. Color and cut out the Gingerbread Baby or the Gingerbread Boy.
2. Using glue or a stapler, attach the Gingerbread Baby or the Gingerbread Boy to a tongue depressor or craft stick.
3. Using a permanent black marker, draw a rectangular shape on one side of the carton and color it in. Add a handle to resemble an oven door.
4. Insert the tongue depressor puppet through the slit into the bottom of the carton.
5. Move the stick up and down to make the Gingerbread Baby or Boy pop out of the oven.

Gingerbread Person Magnet or Ornament
Materials
- brown craft foam or tagboard
- markers, crayons, craft paint
- one picture of each student
- yarn or magnetic tape
- gingerbread people patterns (page 78)
- buttons and beads
- glue
- utility knife

Teacher Preparation
1. Trace the gingerbread pattern onto the craft foam or tagboard and cut it out.
2. Using a utility knife, cut a small oval shape from the face area of the gingerbread person.
3. Glue each student's picture to the back of a gingerbread pattern so that his or her face shows through.

Directions to Students
1. Decorate the gingerbread person, using markers, crayons, paint, buttons, etc.
2. To make an ornament, attach a loop of yarn to the top of the gingerbread person.
3. Place a small strip of magnetic tape on the back to create a magnet.

Gingerbread Art *(cont.)*

Running Gingerbread Boy Book
(Sliding Strip Book)

Materials

- 8½" x 11" (22 cm x 28 cm) light colored construction paper, one per student
- gingerbread boy pattern, page 78, one per student
- markers or crayons
- tagboard
- scissors
- utility knife
- glue

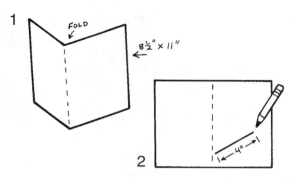

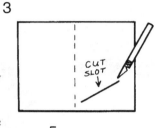

Directions

1. Fold the piece of construction paper in half (hamburger style), then open it again.

2. Draw a line, approximately 4" (10 cm), diagonally upward across the right-hand side of your paper.

3. Cut the line with a utility knife. This is your large slot.

4. Cut a small vertical slot 1 ⅛" (3 cm) long near the end of the large slot.

5. Color and cut out the gingerbread boy pattern (page 78).

6. Create a sliding strip to help the gingerbread boy run across the page by cutting a piece of tagboard 5½" x ¾" (14 cm x 2 cm). Cut a tab 1½" x ¼" (4 cm x .6 cm), using tagboard. Glue the bottom half of the tab to the left side of your strip. Fold the rest of the tab down on itself.

7. Slip the strip through the small slot. Pull the loose part of the tab through the large slot. Fold the end of the tab upward on the tab's fold line. Make sure the fold line of your tab is on the large slot.

8. Apply glue to the top of your folded tab. Place your gingerbread boy on the glued tab (make sure you do not glue your figure to the page). Allow glue to dry before pulling the strip.

9. Cut the end of your strip to make it shorter, if necessary. Your gingerbread boy should now move easily up and down the large slot of your paper. Have children draw other characters from the story (chasing the gingerbread boy) on the left side of the paper.

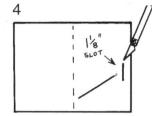

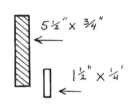

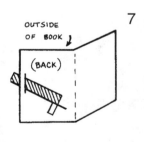

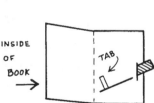

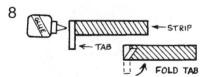

Gingerbread Art

Bottle of Fun

Materials for One Bottle

- one empty 20 oz. (600 mL) soda or water bottle
- gingerbread men mini-erasers
- beads and glitter
- iridescent Easter grass
- $\frac{1}{3}$ cup (80 mL) light corn syrup
- small plastic animals (same as in story)
- hot glue gun
- water

Directions

1. Pour the corn syrup into the jar.
2. Alternately place mini erasers, Easter grass, and small plastic animals in the bottle.
3. Fill the bottle with water.

Teacher Note: When the bottle is full, carefully hot glue the cap onto the bottle.

Painting with Molasses

Materials

- molasses
- ground ginger
- white glue
- 9" x 9" (23 cm x 23 cm) white construction paper, one per child
- copy of Tasty Treats (page 79), one per child
- paintbrushes, crayons, and scissors
- assortment of colored construction-paper triangles for the house roof (one per child); the triangles should each have one 9" (23 cm) side.

Directions for Students

1. Drizzle glue just inside the border of the white construction paper square (to resemble icing). Allow the glue to dry completely. It will be bumpy.
2. Quickly wet the entire paper square by running it under water. Paint the wet paper with molasses and sprinkle it with ginger. Hang it up to dry. (Hint: Place old newspapers under the drying rack to catch the drips.)
3. Glue the triangular roof to the square to form a house.
4. Color and cut out the Tasty Treats patterns (page 79). Glue on the Tasty Treats to decorate the gingerbread house.

58

Gingerbread Art (cont.)

Non-Edible Mini Cutouts

Materials

- 1 cup (225 g) cinnamon
- 1 tablespoon (15 mL) ground cloves
- 1 tablespoon (15 mL) ground nutmeg
- ³/₄ cup (180 mL) applesauce
- 2 tablespoon (30 mL) glue
- cookie cutters
- toothpicks

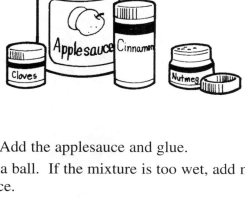

Directions for Students

1. Mix cinnamon, cloves, and nutmeg in a medium bowl. Add the applesauce and glue.
2. Work the mixture with your hands 2–3 minutes to form a ball. If the mixture is too wet, add more cinnamon. If the mixture is too dry, add more applesauce.
3. Lightly dust a clean surface with cinnamon and roll out dough to about ¹/₄" (.6 cm) thickness.
4. Cut out shapes with cookie cutters and use a toothpick to make a hole at the top for hanging.
5. Air dry the cutouts in a sunny spot for 4 or 5 days.

Puffy Gingerbread People

Materials

- 9" x 12" (23 cm x 30 cm) light brown construction paper (two per child)
- Gingerbread Boy patterns, pages 75–76
- scissors
- crayons and colored chalk
- tape and stapler
- newspaper or tissue paper

Teacher Preparation

1. Run two copies of each part of the gingerbread boy pattern for each child. Tape the body parts together so that each child receives the two complete gingerbread boys.
2. Demonstrate to the children how to loosely crumple the newspaper.

Directions to Students

1. Cut out both patterns. Decorate one using crayons or chalk.
2. Place pattern pieces together, with the decorated side on top. Staple or tape them together about three-quarters of the way around.
3. Stuff them with crumpled-up paper. Close the opening.

Gingerbread Art *(cont.)*

Origami Fox

Materials

- 6" x 18" (15 cm x 46 cm) piece of orange construction paper, one per child
- pencils, felt pens

Directions to Students

1. Bring the left edge of the paper to the right edge to fold the paper in half.

2. Using a pencil, make a small dot at the top right edge of the paper about 1" (2.54 cm) from the right corner.

3. Bring the lower right corner up to meet the bottom of the center line and the dot. Crease the paper and open it.

4. Turn the lower right corner up until it meets the creased line.

5. Fold this new flap in half, bringing the lower edge up to the same creased line.

6. Make the fox's ear by turning the flap up and over.

7. Repeat the steps on the left side of the paper.

8. Turn the paper over and draw a face on the fox.

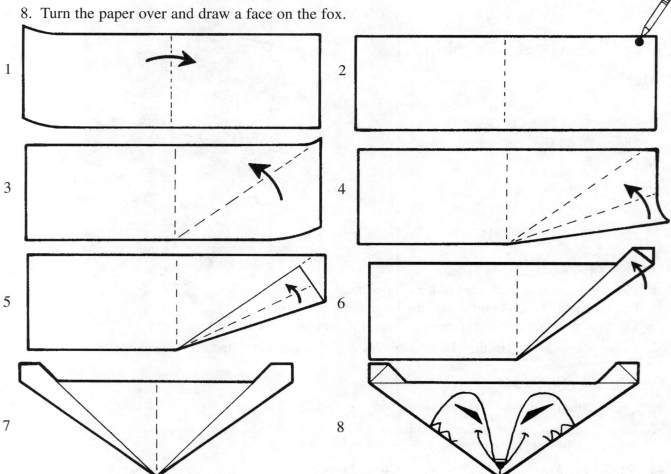

Gingerbread Songs

Come Back Little Man

(sung to the tune of "Five Little Ducks Went Out One Day")

One gingerbread boy popped out one day

Over the hill he ran away.

When the man called, "Come back little man!"

He only answered, "Catch me if you can!"

(Repeat the verse four more times, each time replacing the "man" with a different character from the story—cow, horse, threshers, and mowers.)

(*Last Verse*)

One gingerbread boy popped out one day

Over the hill he ran away.

When the fox called, "Hop on my nose little man!

I'll gobble you up as fast as I can!"

A Gingerbread House

(sung to the tune of "A Hunting We Will Go")

A gingerbread house we'll make,

A gingerbread house we'll make,

With bread, frosting, and some treats

A gingerbread house we'll make.

Let's roll out the dough,

Let's roll out the dough,

We'll cut out a house shape

A gingerbread house we'll make.

We'll squirt on the frosting

We'll squirt on the frosting

Add some candy to decorate

A gingerbread house we'll make.

Gingerbread Recipes

Gingerbread People

Ingredients

Cookies

- 3¼ cups (725 g) all-purpose flour
- ¾ teaspoon (4 mL) baking soda
- ¾ teaspoon (4 mL) salt
- 1 teaspoon (5 mL) ground cinnamon
- 2 teaspoons (10 mL) ground ginger
- ¼ teaspoon (1 mL) ground cloves
- 2 sticks or 1 cup (225 g) butter, softened
- ¼ cup (60 g) dark brown sugar
- 1 large egg
- ½ cup (120 mL) molasses
- gingerbread people cookie cutters

Icing (optional)

- ⅔ cup (160 mL) powdered sugar
- 1–2 teaspoons (5 mL–10 mL) milk

Directions

1. Using an electric mixer, cream butter and sugar in a large bowl. Add the egg and molasses and beat until smooth.

2. Add flour, soda, salt, cinnamon, ginger, and cloves. Blend on low speed just until combined. Do not overmix.

3. Separate the dough into two balls and flatten them into disks. Place each disk in a plastic bag and refrigerate them for one hour or until firm.

4. Roll the dough onto a floured surface with a rolling pin until it is about ¼" (.6 cm) thick. Cut out gingerbread people, using cutters.

5. Place on an ungreased cookie sheet. Bake for 9–11 minutes at 325° F. Remove the cookies from the oven and cool them on a wire rack.

6. If desired, decorate the gingerbread people with icing. Mix the milk and sugar together and spoon the icing into a pastry bag fitted with a small piping tip.

Gingerbread Recipes *(cont.)*

Basic Gingerbread Dough

(Use for the Giant Gingerbread Cookie on page 70.)

Ingredients

- 8 cups (1 kg) flour
- 1½ teaspoons (8 mL) ground cinnamon
- 2¼ cups (560 g) solid vegetable shortening
- 2 eggs
- ⅔ cup (160 mL) light corn syrup

- 2 teaspoons (10 mL) ground ginger
- 1 teaspoon (5 mL) ground cloves
- 2 cups (500 g) sugar
- 1 cup (250 mL) molasses

Directions

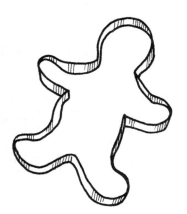

1. Beat the shortening and sugar together with an electric mixer until fluffy. Add the eggs, molasses, and corn syrup. Beat until combined.

2. Gradually add flour, ginger, cinnamon, and cloves. Beat well. If necessary, stir in the last 2 cups (500g) of flour with a wooden spoon. Knead the dough until smooth.

3. Roll out a portion of the dough to a ¼" (6 cm) on a greased rectangular baking pan. Use patterns or cookie cutters to cut out the shapes.

4. Bake at 375° F (190° C) for 10–12 minutes. Let it cool for 5 minutes on the pan. Transfer the cookie to a wire rack and cool.

Gingersnaps

Ingredients

- 2½ cups (550 g) flour
- ¼ teaspoon (1 mL) salt
- 1 teaspoon (5 mL) diced crystallized ginger
- ½ teaspoon (2 mL) ground black pepper
- 1½ sticks butter, softened
- ¼ cup (60 mL) molasses

- ½ teaspoon (2 mL) baking soda
- 2 teaspoons (10 mL) ground ginger
- ½ teaspoon (2 mL) allspice
- 1¼ cups (275 g) dark brown sugar
- 1 large egg

Directions

1. Combine the flour, soda, salt, ground ginger, crystallized ginger, allspice, and pepper in a medium bowl. Mix well with a wire whisk. Set aside.

2. Cream the sugar and butter with an electric mixer in a large bowl. Add the egg and the molasses, and beat until fluffy.

3. Add the flour mixture and mix until combined. Do not overmix. Chill the dough for 1 hour.

4. Form the dough into 1" (2.54 cm) balls. Place the balls onto an ungreased cookie sheet.

5. Bake for 20–25 minutes at 300° F (150° C). Immediately transfer cookies to a wire rack to cool.

Gingerbread Recipes *(cont.)*

Foxy Villain Treat

Ingredients (per child)

- slice of bread
- peanut butter
- 2 raisins
- ¼ banana
- 1 red grape
- 2 apple wedges

Directions

1. Cut the bread into a circle, using a glass as a guide. (See illustration.)

2. Spread peanut butter on the bread circle.

3. Place the banana toward bottom of circle so that it juts out from the face. Place the red grape on top of the banana.

4. Add raisins for eyes and place the two apple wedges at the top of the head for ears.

Gingerbread Pudding People

Ingredients

- 1 package (6-serving size) butterscotch pudding
- ¾ cup (150 g) butter
- ¾ cup (150 g) firmly packed brown sugar
- 1 egg
- 2¼ cups (550 mL) all-purpose flour
- 1 teaspoon (5 mL) baking soda
- 1 tablespoon (15 mL) ground ginger
- 1½ teaspoons (8 mL) ground cinnamon

Directions

1. Cream the dry pudding mix, the butter, and the sugar in a medium bowl. Add the egg and blend well.

2. Combine the flour, baking soda, ginger, and cinnamon.

3. Blend the dry ingredients into the pudding mixture.

4. Chill the dough until firm.

5. Roll out the dough on a floured board to about 1/4" (0.5 cm) thick. Cut with a cookie cutter.

6. Use a straw to make a hole at the top for hanging, if desired.

7. Place the cookies on a greased cookie sheet and bake them at 350° F (180° C) for 10–12 minutes. Remove the cookies from the oven and cool them on a wire rack.

Gingerbread Games

Character Game (Who's Who?)

Materials

- 6" x 18" (15 cm x 46 cm) tagboard strip
- copy of the Character Cards (page 17)
- scissors
- large paper clip
- stapler
- markers or crayons

Teacher Preparation

1. Staple the ends of the tagboard strip together to create a headband. Place the paper clip on the front side of the headband.
2. Color, cut out, and laminate the Character Cards.

Directions

1. Choose one child to be "It." Place the headband on that child and stand him or her in front of the class.
2. Place one character card under the paper clip on the headband.
3. The child wearing the headband chooses one classmate at a time (three in total) to give a clue about the character named on the card.
4. The child wearing the headband is allowed three guesses to correctly name the character. After the three guesses, it is someone else's turn.

Variation: The child wearing the headband can ask questions about the character and his or her classmates can give *yes* or *no* answers to the questions.

Character Match

Materials

- Character Cards (page 17)
- scissors
- markers or crayons

Teacher Preparation

1. Run 2–4 copies of the Character Cards per pair of students.
2. Color, cut out, and laminate the Character Cards sets.

Directions

1. Have children work in pairs. Lay the cards facedown on a flat surface.
2. One child turns over two cards. If the two cards match, the child may keep the pair and then take another turn. If a match is not made, the cards are turned facedown again and the other child takes a turn.
3. This alternating continues until all matches are found. The child with the most matches wins!

Jump Rope Rhymes & Games

Cookies for Sale

Gingerbread cookies up for sale
Great with tea or in a lunch pail.
Shapes of bells, and stars, and men
How much money will you spend?
(1, 2, 3, ... Count the jumps.)

Decorate the House

Decorate the house using chocolate chips,
Cinnamon, cereal, and candy sticks.
Bright colors, light colors, quiet as a mouse.
How many candies to decorate the house?
(1, 2, 3, ... Count the jumps.)

Gingerbread Boy, Gingerbread Boy, Fox!

(played like Duck, Duck, Goose)

Directions

1. Seat children in a circle. Choose one child to walk around the outside of the circle, carefully tapping each sitting child on the head while at the same time calling out, "Gingerbread Boy," as he or she taps each head. Finally, the child taps a head and yells, "Fox!" instead of Gingerbread Boy.

2. When "Fox" is called, the child who was tapped on the head jumps up, leaving an empty spot in the circle, and runs around the circle, trying to catch the child who tapped him or her on the head.

3. The first child back to the open spot sits down in the spot. The other child becomes "It."

Candy Stick Relay

Materials

- 3–4 paper towel tubes
- red tempera paint
- paintbrushes

Teacher Preparation

1. Paint each tube with red stripes to resemble a peppermint stick. Allow the paint to dry.
2. Mark out a small circular course for the children to use as a track.

Directions

1. Divide the class into teams. Space the children at even distances around the track.
2. Give each starting runner a "candy stick" and begin the race. As each child comes to his or her teammate, he or she hands-off the candy stick. This continues until everyone has had a turn.

Variation: Divide the class into two teams. Half of each team lines up at one end of the classroom or field, while the rest of the team lines up directly across from their own team. Give a candy stick to each team to begin the race. Each child holding the candy stick runs across the room or field to his or her own teammates. He or she then passes the stick to the next teammate, who runs back across the room or field passing the candy stick to the next teammate. This continues until the all the children have run.

Gingerlinks

Connect to the Internet and explore these web sites.

Annie's Gingerbread Page

http://www.annieshomepage.com/gingerbread.html

This gingerbread enthusiast gives a brief history of ginger and recipes for gingerbread cakes and ornaments.

Christmas Gingerbread

http://www.ga.k12.pa.us/Academics/LS/2/ginger/Index.html

This site offers a history of gingerbread while showing photos of a 2nd–3rd grade class making gingerbread houses.

The History of Gingerbread

http://www.jollyoldelf.com/gingerbreadhistory.html

Here, you will find the history behind gingerbread along with some neat facts. Recipes are also given along with some background information on the ginger plant.

Necco Gingerbread House

http://www.necco.com/gingerhouse

The Necco candy company has paired up with baking instructor Susan Logozzo to offer a step-by-step guide for creating a gingerbread house using Necco candies. Colorful candy pictures accompany the instructions.

Nabisco Recipes

http://www.nabiscorecipes.com

The Nabisco recipe site offers an easy way to make a gingerbread house using their graham crackers (used when creating this unit's mini-book).

Quick and Easy Graham Cracker Gingerbread House

http://www.onenorthpole.com/MrsClaus/FunFood.html

One North Pole offers a simple way to create a gingerbread house with graham crackers and with other fun food crafts.

Santaland Christmas Recipes

http://www.santaland.com

This site offers information on Christmas traditions, crafts, and food. A special section has been reserved for gingerbread.

Taste of Cyberspace—A History of Gingerbread

http://wwwiz.com/issue04/wiz_d04.html

Learn about the origins of gingerbread and discover the roots for the tradition of gingerbread houses. This site also features recipes and links to other gingerbread resources.

Web Sites

Gingerbread Facts

Connect to *http://www.jollyoldelf.com/gingerbreadhistory.html* to answer these questions.

1. Gingerbread has been baked in Europe for centuries. In some places, it was a soft, spiced cake; in others, a crisp, flat cookie. It became a popular delicacy at carnivals in England. Because of this, the carnivals were called

   _____.

2. Some villages in England require unmarried women to eat gingerbread
   "_____" if they are to stand a chance of
   meeting a real one.

3. If you lived in London in 1614, your family would have gone to the
   _____ on August 24,
   honoring the patron saint, St. Bartholomew. His name might have been
   stamped into your gingerbread.

4. Germany has the longest and strongest tradition of gingerbread. The
   German word for gingerbread is _____.

5. _____ is a famous German
   fairy tale about two children who had been left in the woods by their parents,
   and how they discovered a house made of bread and candy.

6. All ginger comes from a twisted rhizome called
   a ginger root. This thick root is sometimes
   called a _____
   because it can look like one with strange
   fingers.

#3101 Thematic Unit–Gingerbread   68   © *Teacher Created Materials, Inc.*

A Gingerbread Boy Hunt

Materials

- gingerbread cookies

Teacher Preparation

1. Prior to this activity, ask school personnel (nurse, cafeteria staff, secretary, guidance counselor, and principal) to help in the hunt.

2. If you made the child-size gingerbread boy on page 6, Setting the Stage, # 4, it needs to be removed before this activity begins.

Directions

1. For the hunt, gather the children together and tell them that you saw the Gingerbread Boy run by their classroom that morning.

2. Ask the children if they would like to go on a hunt to try to find him.

3. Visit the people (school personnel) helping you. Have the children ask if they have seen the Gingerbread Boy. The person should answer with a *"No, but maybe he went by when I wasn't looking"* or you may wish to have a note (clue) for them to give to the children to lead them on to the next person.

4. Move the children on until they reach the second-to-last adult, preferably the school secretary. Have the children ask their question. This time the adult is to answer, *"No, but I think* _____(the principal's name)_____ *has seen him!"* Children go to the principal's office and ask their question. His or her response will be *"Yes, I have seen the Gingerbread Boy, and he left this treat for you!"* (Have the child-size Gingerbread Boy waiting there, too.) The principal then gives each child a gingerbread cookie.

Gingerbread Goodies

Simple Gingerbread Houses

(Adult volunteers will be needed to help with this activity.)

Materials

- graham crackers, nine per child
- assorted candies
- copies of mini-book, pages 36–40
- canned frosting
- parent letter, page 73
- small meat trays or pieces of foil-covered cardboard

Teacher Preparation

(prior to the event)

1. Send home the note on page 73 asking parents to supply one of the foods necessary to complete this project.
2. Arrange for adult volunteers to assist children.

Directions

The children will love making their own gingerbread houses. Have them reread their mini-books and use them as guides for creating their houses.

Hints:

1. Build houses on small foam meat trays for easy transporting.
2. Make your own pastry bags for the frosting, using self-sealing freezer bags. Place frosting in the bag. Using scissors, clip one of the bottom corners away (very small clip). Squeeze out the frosting.

A Giant Gingerbread Cookie

(Adult volunteers will be needed to help with this activity.)

Materials

- gingerbread recipe, page 63
- Gingerbread Boy pattern, pages 75–76
- rectangular cookie sheet

Directions

1. Create a giant gingerbread cookie. Use the two-part Gingerbread Boy pattern as a template.
2. Using the gingerbread recipe, bake 2–3 pans of dough.
3. Lay the baked gingerbread on a new sheet of butcher paper. Lay the templates on the gingerbread and cut out the gingerbread. Remove the excess.
4. Fasten the gingerbread pieces together with frosting.
5. Allow the children to help decorate the gingerbread boy, using frosting, raisins, candies, and cereal.
6. Enjoy eating this yummy treat!

Variation: Draw a child-size gingerbread boy enlarging the pattern on butcher paper to use as a template. Make 8–10 pans of cookie dough, as needed, to cover the template.

Gingerbread Bulletin Boards

Gingerbread Kids

This bulletin board utilizes the Gingerbread Kids your children created (page 10, #9). Make this child-made bulletin board after teaching the origin of gingerbread to your class. Make an Earth shape by enlarging the pattern on page 54 onto tagboard. Color and cut out the Earth. Mark the origin of gingerbread (North America) and gingerbread houses (Germany) using a marker. Staple four to five Gingerbread Kids, holding hands, across the Earth. Use the remaining Gingerbread Kids as extra border or as a garland in classroom.

Our Gingerbread Village

Creating this three-dimensional bulletin board is simple with the help from your children's families. Plan ahead by collecting clean, dry, student milk cartons. Cut a door into each carton, using a utility knife. Cut it on three sides so that the door can be opened and closed. Make the door large enough to be able to place a small gingerbread cookie inside (page 62). Place each milk carton into a paper lunch bag, and staple the Family Fun letter (page 73) to the outside. Send a bag home with each child. Use butcher paper or construction paper to create the background. As the decorated cartons come in, begin creating your village by stapling them to the bulletin board.

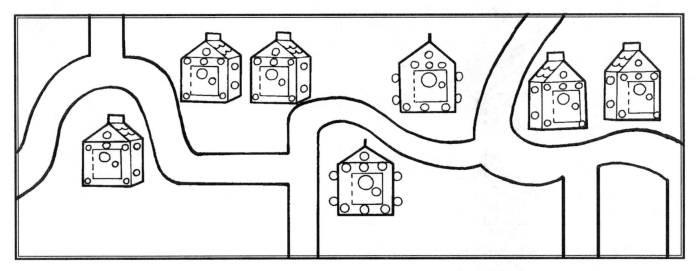

It's Not Just for the Holidays!

Many times when people hear the word "gingerbread," the winter holidays come to mind. And, although this would be a wonderful unit to incorporate during the holidays, it can also be a great way to kick off the school year!

A Gingerbread Boy Hunt!

Take your children on a Gingerbread Boy Hunt (page 69). This activity will give you the opportunity to introduce the children to many of the school staff members.

Where Do I Live?

Learning an address is difficult for many children. Ask the children's caretakers to participate in the Family Fun activity (page 73). Label each "house" with the child's address. Review the addresses with children on a regular basis.

Math Manipulatives

Simple subtraction and spatial relationships, math concepts generally covered or reviewed near the beginning of the school year, can be made fun with the use of the work mat (page 28–29). Make mini-gingerbread counters or use teddy graham crackers as manipulatives.

Let's Talk Manners

Let's face it, the Gingerbread Baby is rather bold and brassy! This would be the perfect time for discussing classroom, school, and friendship rules.

Family Fun Letter

Date _____

Dear Parents,

We are studying a unit on gingerbread and we have two special requests. First, we would like to create a three-dimensional Gingerbread Village bulletin board for our classroom, but we need your help! In this bag you will find one milk carton, already washed and dried. We need your family's help to turn it into a gingerbread house. Please cover the carton by painting it brown or by using this brown paper bag. The roof may be colored a different color. Next, glue on macaroni, buttons, beans, beads, glitter, fabric scraps, etc., to decorate it. Have fun and be creative! Please return your family's creation by _____.

Second, as our gingerbread unit comes to an end, our class will be making simple gingerbread houses. Each child is being asked to bring in one item to help share with the cost of this special project.

Please send in _____

with your child by _____.

Thank you for your time and help.

Sincerely,

_____
                Teacher

Gingerbread Baby Patterns

74

Large Gingerbread Boy Pattern

Directions: Cut out the patterns on pages 75 and 76. Connect the body parts at the dotted line using tape (on the back.)

Large Gingerbread Boy Pattern *(cont.)*

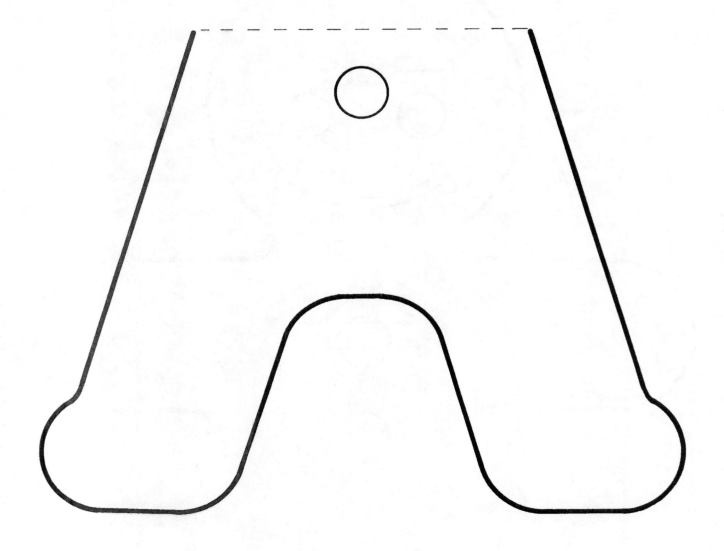

Gingerbread House Pattern

Gingerbread People Patterns

Tasty Treat Patterns

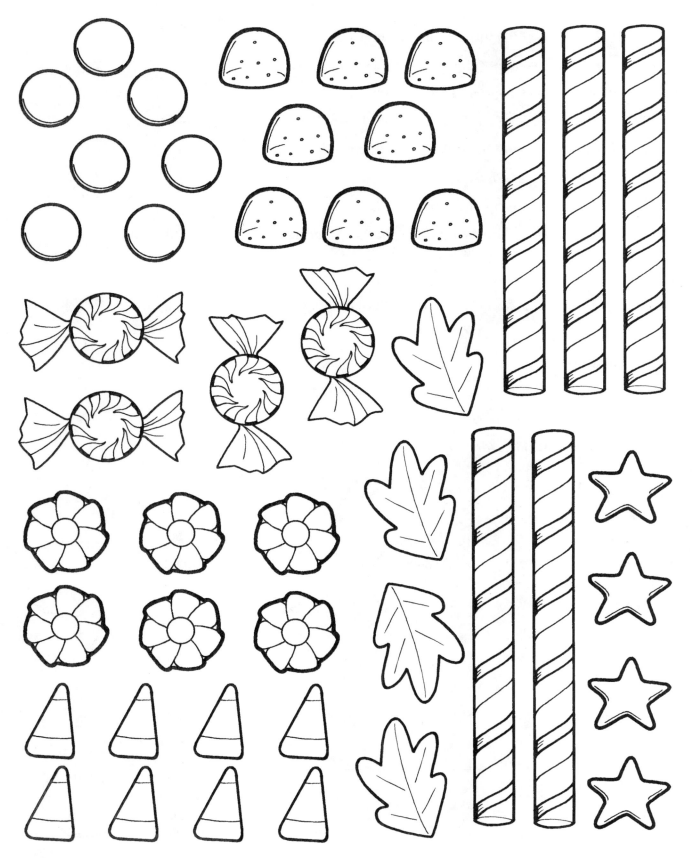

Bibliography

Amoss, Berthe. *The Cajun Gingerbread Boy.* MTC Press, 1999.

Bracken, Carolyn. *Easy-to-Make: Gingerbread House.* Dover Publications, 1991.

Brett, Jan. *Gingerbread Baby.* Penguin Putnam Books for Young Readers, 1999.

Cousins, Lucy. *Maisy Makes Gingerbread.* Candlewick Press, 1999.

Egielski, Richard. *The Gingerbread Boy.* Harper Collins, 1997.

Galdone, Paul. *The Gingerbread Boy.* Clarion Books, 1983.

Jarrell, Randall. *The Gingerbread Rabbit.* HarperCollins Children's Books, 1995.

Lesser, Rika. *Hansel and Gretel.* Dutton Books, 1999.

McDougall, Scott. *Peek-a-Boo Gingerbread House.* Grosset & Dunlap, 1997.

McGraw-Hill, Inc. *The Gingerbread Fudd (Junior Academic Series)* McGraw-Hill Consumer Products, 1999.

Mell, Randy. *My Gingerbread House.* Fun Works Publishing, 1997.

Rowe, John A. *The Gingerbread Man.* North-South Books, 1998.

Santoro, Christopher. *Who's in My Gingerbread House?* Random House, Inc., 1995.

Takayama, Sandi. *The Musubi Man: Hawaii's Gingerbread Man.* Island Book Shelf, 1997.

Tews, Susan. *The Gingerbread Doll.* Clarion Books, 1993.

Thomas, Carol. *Gingerbread Days.* HarperTrophy Children's Books, 1997.

Zeifert, Harriet. *The Gingerbread Boy.* Econo-Clad Books, 1999.

Answer Key

Page 15

(correct order)

1. wheat field
2. mowers
3. threshers
4. mill-flour
5. mixing bowl
6. gingerbread cookie

Page 51

2 + 3 = 5	4 + 2 = 6
1 + 2 = 3	3 + 1 = 4
4 + 3 = 7	2 + 2 = 4
5 + 2 = 7	3 + 3 = 6
1 + 1 = 2	2 + 4 = 6

Page 30

Mystery Word: ice

Page 50

1. 5
2. 6
3. 5
4. 7

Page 68

1. Gingerfairs
2. husbands
3. Bartholomew Fair
4. Lebkuchen
5. Hansel and Gretel
6. hand